AF406101

MONGOL
EMPIRE

A BRIEF HISTORY FROM BEGINNING TO END

HISTORY HUB

Bonus Downloads

*Get Free Books with **<u>Any Purchase</u>** History Hub*

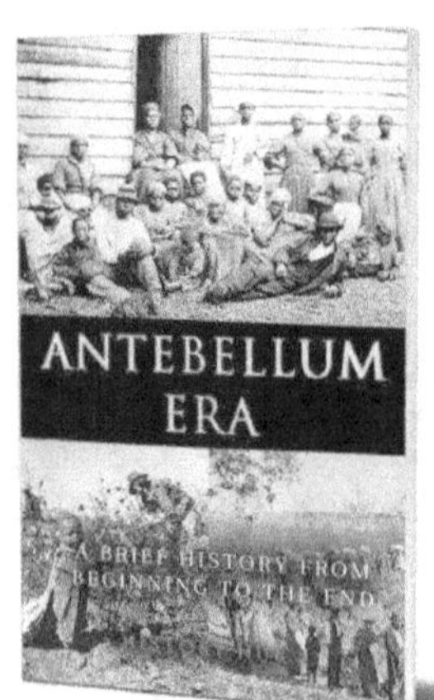

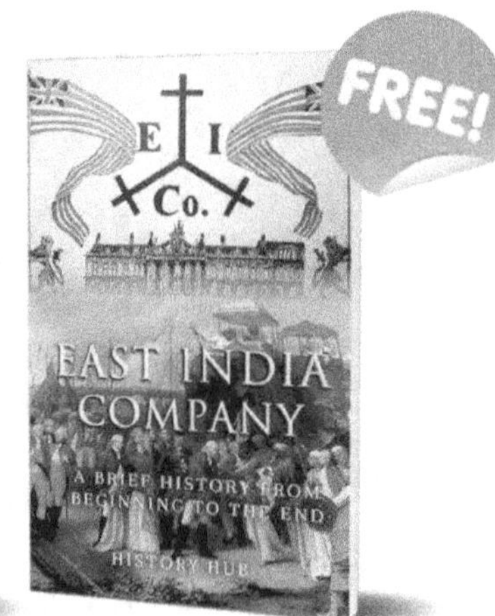

Every purchase comes with a FREE download!

or Click Here.

Scan Your Phone to open QR code

Mongol Empire

A Brief History from Beginning to the End

History Hub

© 2022 Copyright by History Hub. All Rights Reserved.

Please Note: The book you are about to enjoy is an analytical review meant for educational and entertainment purposes as an unofficial companion. If you have not yet read the original work, please do before purchasing this copy.

Disclaimer & Terms of Use: No part of this publication may be reproduced or retransmitted, electronic or mechanical, without the written permission of the publisher. The information in this book is meant for educational and entertainment purposes only and the publisher and author make no representations or warranties with respect to the accuracy or completeness of these contents and disclaim all warranties such as warranties of fitness for a particular purpose. Product names, logos, brands, and other trademarks featured or referred to within this publication are the property of their respective trademark holders and are not affiliated with this publication. This is an unofficial summary and analytical review meant for educational and entertainment purposes only and has not been authorized, approved, licensed, or endorsed by the original book's author or publisher and any of their licensees or affiliates.

CONTENTS

Chapter One
Introduction

The Fascinating History of the Mongolian Empire

Kubla Khan

by Samuel Taylor Coleridge - 1772-1834

In Xanadu did Kubla Khan

A stately pleasure dome decree:

Where Alph, the sacred river, ran

Through caverns measureless to man

Down to a sunless sea.

Samuel Taylor Coleridge wrote the poem about Kublai Khan, published in 1816. It was written about the great hero and grandson of Genghis Khan while Coleridge was in an opium-induced dream. The poem describes the legendary and great capital city of Xanadu which was, as history has it, built by Kublai Khan.

This serves to remind us of the great sense of mystery and wonder which has always risen in the minds of people when they read or think about Genghis Khan and the more romantic figure of Kublai Khan.

Mongolia is a country situated in the northern part of Central Asia, landlocked between China and Russia. It also has a very dry and harsh climate set high on plateaus and dominated by the Gobi Desert. It has unique flora and fauna and some particularly rare and interesting animals including the noteworthy Gobi bear, which is, unfortunately, critically endangered.

Mongolia has a fascinating history and a long prehistory. While the Empire of Mongolia was formed by the tribal chieftain Genghis Khan in 1206, the country previously had a long history of tribal squabbles. There is a strong possibility that these militant tribesmen were originally what we call the Huns, although they were dominant nearly 1000 years before the formation of the Mongolian Empire. The Huns, like the Mongols, were a nomadic people from Central Asia who fought on horseback and were terrifyingly accurate archers. The first mention of them is made about 221 BC. The Romans also had their run-ins with the Huns. They settled on the plains of Hungary, but they were permanently skirmishing with the Romans, and in 441 AD, Attila the Hun, of fearsome repute, attacked Constantinople and was thus given the name, "scourge of God." After his death, however, the Hunnic Empire collapsed and fragmented tribes were all that remained. Historians believe that, as the Huns came from the same area that the Mongols did and that they were similar in appearance, particularly before they moved West into Europe, it is possible that they were the ancestors of the Mongolian tribesmen.

When Genghis Khan united the tribes to form the Empire of Mongolia, it was the beginning of a dramatic and bloody period in history. Within less than two hundred years, they had created a huge empire that encompassed large parts of Russia, China, the Middle East, and Central Asia. It was ruled by Genghis Khan and his descendants, and it is estimated that they were responsible for the death of more than 40 million people, shrinking the world population at that time by 11%.

After the collapse and fragmentation of the Mongolian Empire, Northern Mongolia was finally colonized in 1691 by the Manchu (Qing) dynasty in China. In 1911, the Qing rule collapsed in Mongolia and Mongolia's religious leader, Bogd Khan, was made head of state. Independence was not achieved immediately, and it was only with the help of Russian troops that the Mongolian People's Republic was formed in 1924.

Until the end of 1980, Mongolia was a one-party state with very close links to the Soviet Union, and it adopted standard communist principles of government. In 1990, however, changing thinking ended the Communist one-party state and brought in an era of a multiparty democracy and a constitution that allowed for more freedom of culture, religion, and trade.

It's perfectly understandable that the proud nomadic people who had a history of riding beautiful horses, of warfare, of galloping through the desert, of close family communities living in yurts, and sharing colorful shamanistic religious experiences would have found their years under the gray drudgery of communist philosophy extremely restrictive and that they would have been anxious and excited to bring their own colorful culture and their own freedom to express themselves in their religious and cultural beliefs back into their lives.

We'll take a brief look at modern Mongolia before we lose ourselves in the fascinating history of one of the most magnificent empires to ever have existed.

Chapter Two
Modern Mongolia - Where is it?

Before we begin our discussion on the fascinating history of Mongolia, we should have a brief look at where it is and who the Mongolian people are. An understanding of geography is important to be able to appreciate how difficult it was to create an empire in such harsh conditions.

Modern Mongolia is located in Asia, sandwiched between Russia in the north and China in the south. It's a very beautiful country nestled on high mountains, with people living on the plateaus. It's actually one of the world's highest countries, situated at an astounding 1,580 meters (5,182 feet) above sea level. It's only about 700 km from the Yellow Sea, although it's so high above it. It's also a huge country that is very sparsely populated. In a country covering more than 1,564,000 square kilometers, it has a population of just over 3,300,000.

Mongolia has very extreme and variable temperatures, which can differ by up to 35 degrees in one single day. It's definitely a country that has many seasons in one day. It's also an extremely dry country that has less than 100 mm or 4 inches of rainfall a year.

The Gobi Desert

This immense desert encompasses 1,295,000 square kilometers of land, making it the largest desert in Asia and the fourth biggest in the world. Lying in a remote area, with Siberia in the north, its relative proximity to the North Pole makes it the world's coldest desert.

It's not a romantic, fascinating desert with lots of picturesque sand dunes and palm-dotted oases. It consists of hard rocky land, but this barren landscape aided travel across the desert, making it a significant trade route from the earliest times. The name Gobi directly translates to "very large and dry," which pretty much describes it in a nutshell. The Gobi is so dry because it's what weather guys call a rain shadow desert. The Himalayan Mountains stop the rain clouds from reaching the Gobi Desert, so it seldom gets any rain.

The People

We'll be learning a lot about the Mongolian people as we go through their history. Modern Mongolian culture is a mix of Buddhism, Shamanism, and the principles of nomadic values. While the influences of Marxism and socialism are also prevalent in the population, modern-day Mongolians have adopted many of the formal manners and beliefs that many other Asian cultures have.

A meal in Mongolia is usually a casual relaxed affair as it would have been during their nomadic past. Tables are rare, and it is usual to sit on the ground. Guests should sit on their feet ensuring that they are not pointing toward the food on the dining mat. Food is accepted with the right hand and it's considered rude not to try everything on offer, even if it looks a bit odd to you. Mongolians eat a lot of meat cooked in a wok with salt. Usually, food is presented as thick stews with potatoes or dumplings. A cup of black tea called Khar tsai is served before the meal to aid digestion, and vodka or a salty milk drink are usually on offer. The salty milk drink is definitely an acquired taste. And remember that Mongolians admire punctuality, so don't be late if you do get invited to dine with them.

Mongolian Homes

Mongolians have always been keen riders as a nomadic people, but with more and more people moving into towns, these aspects of this nomadic lifestyle are disappearing.

A yurt is a traditional dwelling of a round tent with a wicker frame and animal hide or felt sides. Yurt dwellings or round dwellings, which resemble yurts, are still quite common in Mongolia. Bronze Age cave art shows evidence of yurt homes, which were also used by the Huns between the 4th and 6th centuries.

The ancient nomads would carry their yurts with them and set up new camps three or four times a year. Although they were light, they still required 3 or 4 pack animals to move so they weren't quite the pack-up-and-go type.

Mongolian Culture

The Mongol present is strongly based on its nomadic past and on its ancient religions. The earliest religion was Shamanism, which included ancestor worship and the druidical beliefs in the power of earth, water, and fire.

Kublai Khan converted to Buddhism during his reign, which rendered Tibetan Buddhism the dominant and official religion.

Much of the formal aspects of the Mongolian government, education, and infrastructure are still much as they were at the end of communist times, although there's a definite drift away from those times which were not happy ones for the Mongol people.

Chapter Three
The Beginning of the Great Mongolian Empire

By the early 1400s, the Mongolians had invaded and conquered most of Eurasia. It's fascinating to look at the beginnings of this great achievement. And it all began with a man called Genghis Khan.

In the year 1206, Temüjin, the son of Yesügei, was elected as Genghis Khan, which means extreme ruler. This event must certainly be seen as the beginning of the Mongol Empire. A tribal federation consisting of Mongol-Turkic tribes met on the banks of the Onon River and declared Genghis Khan, who had previously just been a tribal leader, as supreme emperor. Genghis Khan was an undisputed leader even in those early days, which is no doubt why people decided to give in while the going was good and give him their loyalty rather than wait for him to take it.

Genghis Khan - the Man

As a child, Genghis Khan was raised tough. The brutality of Steppe life meant that only the tough would survive. His father was killed by poison when Genghis Khan was only nine, and the tribe then expelled his mother and her seven children. The fight for survival was enormous, and the young Genghis Khan became an effective hunter, although it's possible he murdered his half-brother in a food related dispute, which takes sibling rivalry to a new level. He and his wife were also abducted by a rival clan and kept as slaves until he escaped.

Genghis Khan carried out an extensive series of campaigns. Between 1205 and 1208, Genghis Khan had attacked most of China and when Beijing fell in 1225, most of the territory north of the Yellow River already belonged to the Mongol Empire. By 1218, East Turkestan acquiesced to the Mongols. The advance continued into Southern Russia and Crimea. By the time Genghis Khan died in 1227, the empire was spread from the China Sea in the East, the Caspian Sea in the west, Tibet to the south, and Siberia in the north. His son Ögödei was chosen to follow him.

Unbelievable Facts About Genghis Khan

According to historical estimates, Genghis Khan was responsible for as many as 40 million people dying. Middle Ages censuses showed the plummeting of the Chinese population by ten million, and it is believed that during the battle with the Iranian Khwarezmid Empire, three-quarters of the population might have lost their lives. It's estimated that Mongol attacks might have decimated the world population.

On the other hand, Genghis Khan is thought to have fathered such huge numbers of children that about 16 million men today are direct descendants of the great Mongol emperor. This was proved by a study of the genetic markers of the Y chromosome, which showed that these sixteen million Asian men shared Genghis Khan's genetic markers. It goes without saying that there was unlikely to be another male fathering children at that rate, so the credit goes to Genghis Khan. He had six wives and more than five hundred concubines and fathered many hundreds of children.

Genghis Khan's descendants were also prolific breeders. His grandson Kublai Khan added thirty virgins to his harem every year, which meant lots of babies over and above his twenty-two legitimate sons.

Genghis Khan took beautiful women for himself from every conquest. If they did not match up to his exacting standards, he gave them to his soldiers. He particularly favored the wives and daughters of the men he conquered, much as a male lion does to ensure his gene pool endures.

Genghis Khan treated his wives, especially Börte, his first wife, with respect. She had been captured with him when they were teenagers and newlyweds. Genghis rescued her, but she had been raped and abused. There was no certainty that her first son was Genghis Khan's child but he accepted him as his legitimate heir anyhow.

No one knew what Genghis Khan looked like, but it is expected that he would have been tall, robust, and strong with a traditional mane of hair and long, black beard.

Equally, no one actually knows how Genghis Khan died or where he was buried. He is most likely to have died of battlefield injuries, but some sources suggest malaria. Some rumors speculate he was murdered while trying to rape a princess from China, and it is even suggested that she castrated him. He also took great care that his burial place would not be found. His soldiers killed everybody who saw the funeral procession, killed the slaves that buried him and then trampled his grave with their horses till no evidence was left. His tomb was probably on the Burkhan Khaldun Mountain, but no one knows where exactly it is to this day despite efforts to locate it.

Although Genghis Khan is seen as the nation's great hero and the founder of Mongolia, during Soviet rule, the mention of his name was forbidden, and all mention of him was removed from history textbooks. Pilgrimages to his birthplace were forbidden. The Soviets were terrified of the resurgence of Mongolian nationalism. After the Mongolian independence in the 1990s, however, he was revived as a great hero with his face appearing on banknotes and an airport named after him.

Chapter Four
Mongolia 1227 and Beyond

After the death of Genghis Khan, the Mongolian Empire covered an enormous area. It covered the whole region between the China and Caspian seas, the forest area of Siberia, Tibet, and central China. It was a tricky empire to manage consisting of many many different religions, cultures, languages, and civilizations. There had always been enmity among the different tribes and a considerable amount of raiding and retaliation. As we know Genghis Khan's own wife was snatched by a tribe in retaliation for the snatching of his mother years earlier. The steppe dwellers were nomads who ranged freely and considered all they went past to be theirs by right which was frustrating and maddening for the settled agricultural communities who would find their crops and settlements being razed regularly. However, none of these normal patterns of raids and counter raids can begin to explain the dimension and might of the Empire building by Genghis Khan

The Military Might of the Mongolian Empire

One reason for the empire's success could be attributed to the military prowess of the Mongolian army led by Genghis Khan, a successful and advanced strategist who easily defeated the superior numbers of the tribesmen and nations he conquered.

The Mongol armies largely consisted of horsemen who could travel at high speeds and were extremely advanced and superbly trained archers. They only fought in hand-to-hand combat when they had completely disarrayed the enemy.

They were most successful on the open plains, but Genghis Khan was not afraid to learn from his conquered people, and he would use the skills of technologically advanced people whom he had conquered to help him subdue walled cities. The Persian, Arab, and Chinese engineers and artisans were pressed into helping him complete his reign of terror. Genghis Khan also implemented a refined messenger service to ensure that they were never surprised by their enemy and that they themselves maintained the element of surprise.

Diplomacy

Genghis Khan and his descendants used a wide network of propaganda and spies. Before they conquered a territory, they would seek a "diplomatic solution," which meant that they gave its leaders, government, or any deciding body a chance to surrender voluntarily. If they agreed, lives were spared, and they had to bend a knee to the Khan and become obedient to his will and taxes. The men would be incorporated into the Khan's army. Often, very few native Mongolians even made up the vast armed forces that swept across to advance the empire. If the population resisted, retribution was swift and usually meant mass slaughter or enslavement. Often, only those with valuable skills were spared.

The Mongols had a huge and effective network for spying and communication. Genghis Khan created a courier service mounted on fast steeds known as Yam. It involved a series of way stations and posthouses strung across the entire empire. Official riders would rest and take on a fresh horse every few miles, which meant that galloping at full speed, they could often cover more than 200 miles in a single day. This allowed missives, information, and lightweight goods to be carried across the empire at a very high speed during those times. The Yam also acted as

Genghis Khan's information hotspots on the ground, easily relaying any political or military problems which were arising. The Yam also made it possible for tradespeople, merchants, and foreign visitors to travel safely. This service was used by the famous Venetian merchant and writer Marco Polo and John of Plano Carpini who was an archbishop and explorer.

A Portrait of Genghis Khan - According to historical estimates, Genghis Khan was responsible for as many as 40 million people dying. Middle Ages censuses showed the plummeting of the Chinese population by ten million, and it is believed that during the battle with the Iranian Khwarezmid Empire, three-quarters of the population might have lost their lives. It's estimated that Mongol attacks might have decimated the world population.

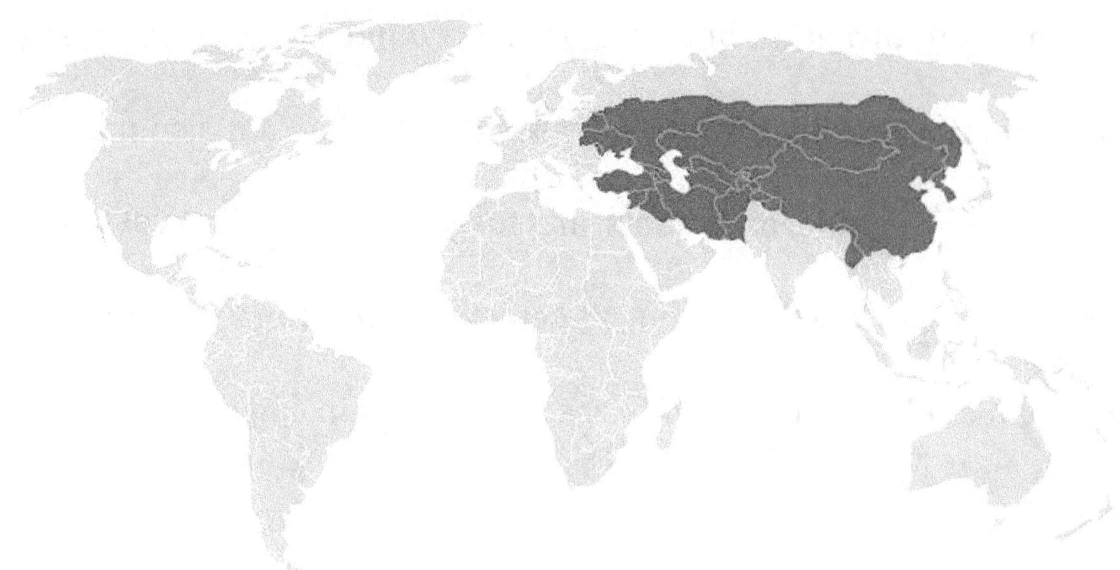

A Map of the Mongolian Empire - By the early 1400s, the Mongolians had invaded and conquered most of Eurasia. It's fascinating to look at the beginnings of this great achievement. And it all began with a man called Genghis Khan.

Chapter Five
The Silk Road

One of the most important results of Genghis Khan's expansive empire with its protected routes that allowed trade to thrive and flourish was what is commonly called the "Silk Road." In existence for more than 1,500 years and consisted of a vast network of routes and roads, it offered merchants, diplomats, explorers, and adventurers an opportunity to trade and exchange ideas and learn about other cultures.

Section 1: What was the Silk Road?

Because the Silk Road was not exactly a road but a vast number of routes, modern historians prefer to call it the "Silk Route." It has been in existence since 130 BC when the Chinese Han dynasty opened a trade route, and it lasted until 1453 AD when the Ottoman Empire in Turkey stopped trading with the West. The Silk Road was coined by the German geographer Ferdinand von Richthofen in 1877, but the name was definitely more romantic than accurate.

Section 2: How was it controlled and maintained?

The Silk Road extended over an impressive 4,000 miles (approximately 6,400 km) across some of the harshest terrains in the world. It stretched across the Pamir Mountains, called the "roof of the world" because of their great height, and across the Gobi Desert, which we have already discussed.

The roads were normally unprotected and in very poor condition except in areas where Genghis Khan's Yam ran. In order to be safe, travelers banded together with their pack animals and formed quite large caravans to protect themselves from robbers. In time, inns and trading posts rose up and offered food, shelter, and protection to the travelers.

A wide variety of merchandise traveled along the Silk Road, particularly silk woven in China and carried to Europe to be purchased by royalty and the very wealthy. Other Asian commodities were precious stones, porcelain, jade, spices, and tea. In exchange, commodities from Europe and the Middle East included textiles, glassware, and an immensely important commodity—horses.

Section 3: Famous Travelers on the Silk Road

As mentioned previously, one of the famous travelers to go along the Silk Road was the Italian merchant, Marco Polo. When he was a young man, he traveled with his father to China, which was then known as Cathay. It took them more than three years to reach the great Kublai Khan in his famous palace Xanadu in 1275. Marco Polo stayed at Kublai Khan's court and was sent on missions all over Asia, visiting places that Europeans had never seen. He then recounted his tales, particularly about the famous Mongolian Khan when he returned to Europe. It was clear that Marco Polo realized the importance of the Silk Road in bringing horses from the West that helped develop the mighty Mongol Empire and bringing gunpowder from the East, which changed the character of wars in Europe. Dreaded diseases like the "Black Death," which devastated Medieval Europe in the 1340s also traveled along the Silk Road from Asia. There is no doubt that the Silk Road was highly instrumental in the development of the Mongolian Empire.

Chapter Six
The Famous Kublai Khan: Early Years

Kublai Khan was the grandson of Genghis Khan, and after he conquered China, he became the first emperor of the Yuan dynasty.

Section 1: Kublai Khan (c. 1215–c. 1294)

In 1260, Kublai Khan became the ruler of the empire established by Genghis Khan, his grandfather. Unlike his grandfather, he was more diplomatic and established a system of rule with a strong administrative bent that respected the local customs and beliefs of the people he had conquered. After he subjugated the Song dynasty in China and established the Yuan dynasty, there was a long, prosperous period of relative peace and growth in Southern China. Unfortunately, in later years, political infighting, prejudicial social policies, and unsuccessful military campaigns would be his undoing.

Section 2: Inheritor of the Empire

Kublai Khan, born as the fourth son of the Mongolian imperial family, was not meant to inherit the great Mongolian Empire. This meant that he was raised in a very traditional manner on the Mongolian steppes and was taught the arts of hunting, riding, and warfare from a young age. He was also, which was unusual for a young Mongolian prince, exposed to Chinese philosophy and culture that would later stir a desire in him to be part of that advanced culture.

Kublai Khan's brother, Möngke, who was the heir, placed Kublai Khan in charge of operations in Northern China when he became Khan in 1251. With respect for Chinese culture and customs, Kublai Khan surrounded himself with Chinese advisors. He did join his brother in extending the empire, but his strategy for conquest was of restraint and respect for his subjects.

Section 3: Emergence into Power

In 1259, Kublai Khan was told that his brother had been killed and that Ariq Böke, his brother and the youngest of the Khans, had called on the great families of Mongolia to name him Great Khan. Kublai Khan was engaged in the battle of Song in the south of China, but he had no intention of letting his brother get away with that. As a result, he brokered a truce with the Song dynasty and went home to Mongolia where he himself was named the Great Khan. The effect of this move was a prolonged civil war between the brothers, but finally, Ariq Böke was roundly beaten in 1264, and his followers were scattered. He surrendered to his brother in Xanadu (Shangdu), and in respect for his blood, Kublai Khan spared his life, but he rounded up and executed all his supporters. He wasn't having his throne threatened a second time, and he was hailed the undisputed Great Khan after that event.

"I have heard that one can conquer the empire on horseback, but one cannot govern it on horseback."

These were apparently the words of one of Kublai Khan's Chinese advisors who saw a major flaw in the politically and diplomatically inexperienced Mongol leaders. In fact, just a few years before Kublai Khan was born, most Mongol tribesmen including their leaders were illiterate. This affected their ability to govern during peace times.

Are You Enjoying Reading?

As an independent publisher

with a tiny marketing budget

we rely on readers, like you.

Click here to a brief review on Amazon

If you're receiving help from this book,

would you please take a moment to write a brief review?

We really appreciate it.

Simply scan QR Code with your Smartphone

Chapter Seven
Kublai Khan: The Later Years

While it's obvious Kublai Khan was a wise and sensible ruler, there were definite flaws in his system of government, which eventually led to the end of Mongolian rule in China.

Section 1: The Wisdom of the Khan

At first, exhibiting a sensible and pragmatic approach, Kublai Khan moved the capital of his empire to Dadu, which is present-day Beijing. He ruled in an administrative rather than a military manner, respecting local customs. During his reign, he showed great religious tolerance, he made significant improvements in infrastructure and he even introduced paper money to use to trade with the West.

He introduced an interesting class system to reinforce the social structure. The Mongolian Aristocracy and the Foreign Merchants did not pay tax and had many special privileges while the Chinese working classes shouldered the whole tax burden and were expected to do a great deal of the enforced manual labor. This unequal system has been pointed out as one of his failings.

Section 2: The Expansion of the Empire

Because his rule was more benevolent and reasonable than that of his grandfather, he was honored with the flattering title the "Wise Khan."

Despite this benevolence, he remained very ambitious, and in 1267, he made another attempt on the sovereignty of the Song dynasty in Southern China. He had left them alone since his civil war with his brother.

It was a difficult campaign as the terrain did not suit the Mongolian horsemen, and the Chinese fought from walled cities. Kublai Khan had to use all sorts of modern war technology, like catapults, to fight back. He also had to significantly increase the size of the navy. Nonetheless in 1279, he finally defeated the Song dynasty and became the first Mongolian to rule the entire country of China.

Kublai Khan's Yuan dynasty was established as a celebration of his great victory. However, it was not a long-lived dynasty as it collapsed in 1368.

Section 3: The Unraveling of the Empire and the Death of the Khan

Kublai Khan's Chinese policies, although they did advantage him in his rule of China, earned him significant criticism among members of the Mongolian Aristocracy who accused him of betraying his Mongolian customs and heritage. His most vocal rival was his cousin, Kaidu, who believed that Kublai Khan's older brother had got his power illegitimately. Kaidu never let the crown rest easy on Kublai Khan's head even though he never overthrew him.

The discrimination that Kublai Khan imposed with his social structure caused increasing resentment among the Chinese citizens of the country. They resented paying for his failed military campaigns in Burma, Java, and Japan.

Kublai Khan had two wives, but he was most fond of his first wife Empress Chabi. He remarried when she died, but her death and that of his eldest son, who was his heir, nearly broke Kublai Khan. He allowed his health to suffer, becoming obese and developing gout from his excesses. When he died in 1294, at the age of 79, he was a broken man.

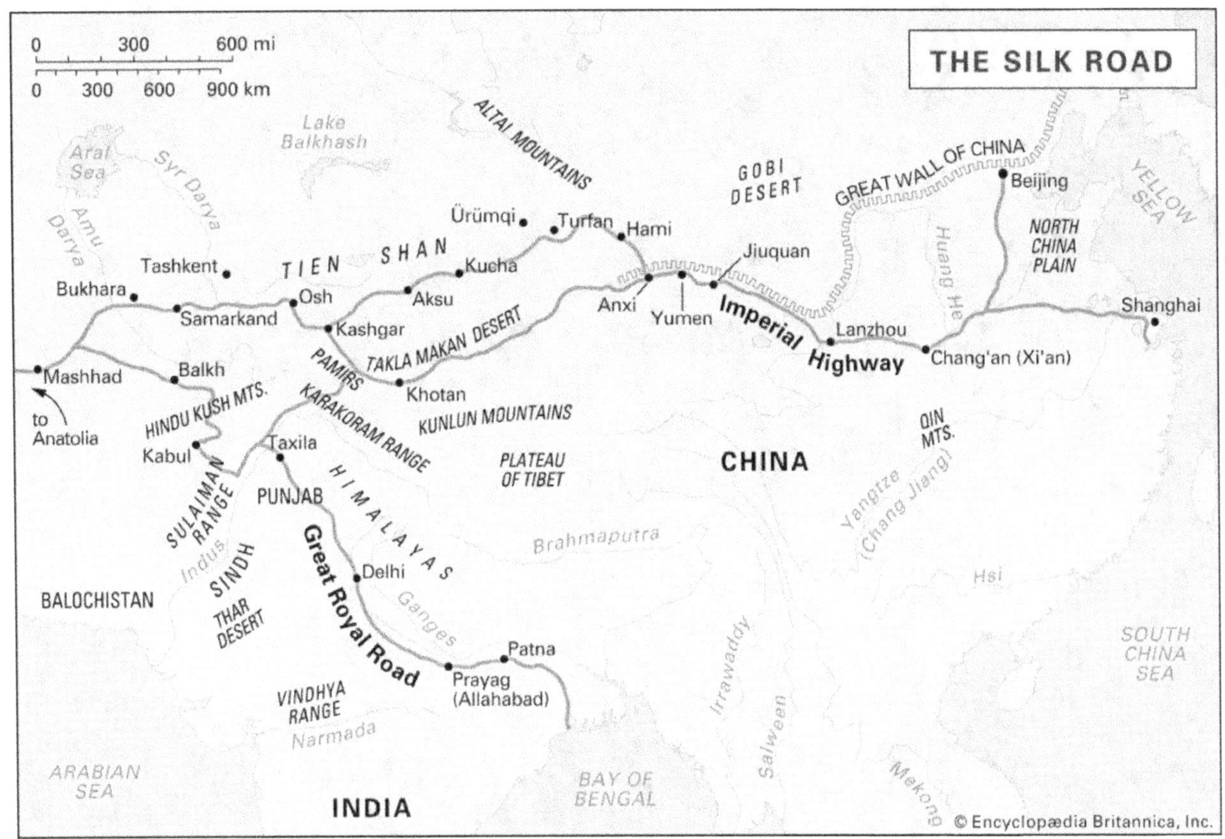

The Silk Road - One of the most important results of Genghis Khan's expansive empire with its protected routes that allowed trade to thrive and flourish was what is commonly called the "Silk Road." In existence for more than 1,500 years and consisted of a vast network of routes and roads, it offered merchants, diplomats, explorers, and adventurers an opportunity to trade and exchange ideas and learn about other cultures.

A Portrait of Kublai Khan - Kublai Khan had two wives, but he was most fond of his first wife Empress Chabi. He remarried when she died, but her death and that of his eldest son, who was his heir, nearly broke Kublai Khan. He allowed his health to suffer, becoming obese and developing gout from his excesses. When he died in 1294, at the age of 79, he was a broken man.

Chapter Eight

The Decline of the Mongols - The Mamluks

Section 1: Reasons for the Decline of the Mongols

Historians have suggested a number of reasons for the decline of the Mongolian Empire.

1. The caliber of leadership declined after the death of the last of the Great Khans.

2. The tax-paying peasant class became resentful of the high-handed Mongolian Aristocracy. Also, they were in vastly greater numbers than their conquerors.

3. The Mongolians resorted to splintering into groups, in-house fighting, and tribal squabbles.

4. The Mongols inadvertently trained their conquered people to fight against them by sharing their skills. Also, the Mongols had become dependent on these people, often from more advanced and skillful civilizations.

5. The essentially nomadic Mongolians struggled to maintain a stable, centralized form of government. It was simply too unwieldy for one person to manage and when administrators or chieftains called Khanates were employed, they could not be trusted to be loyal.

6. The vastly varied cultures of the conquered people made it impossible to allow for social cohesion, particularly in distant cultures like the European ones, which were so unlike their own and so far from their actual seat of government.

All these reasons made it nearly impossible to maintain the empire once the military momentum collapsed.

Section 2: The Defeat of the Mongols in the Middle East by the Mamluks

After the death of Genghis Khan, his kingdom was divided amongst his sons and later was fragmented still further among his grandsons, although this was officially still under the Great Khan. By the time Kublai Khan had set up his seat of government in China, Mongolian control in central Mongolia and other regions was collapsing.

The Mongolian techniques of warfare reliant on cavalry and speed became less effective with the introduction of more effective and advanced weapons and gunpowder.

Section 3: The Battles with the Mamluks

By mid-1300s, the Mongolian forces were just about to defeat Jerusalem when they were resisted by the Mamluks, a group of Muslim-owned Arab slaves from Egypt. They were a type of unpaid mercenary used by their Arab masters to fight. They were the world's most skilled soldiers, fearsome horsemen with huge curved swords.

They held high rank and very privileged positions when they were not at war. Some became independent and formed their own dynasties, fighting right from the 1300s and for many centuries thereafter. They even fought Napoleon Bonaparte's formidable French army. They defeated the Mongol army in Palestine in 1260. They were aided by free passage across Christian land by the Crusaders. This was unexpected because it was thought that the Crusaders might help the Mongolians to attack Muslim-occupied Jerusalem.

The Mamluk sultan routed the Mongolian troops at Ain Jalut and went on to destroy strongholds in the area. The Mongol hold on the Middle East was broken despite their retaliation, destroying Damascus. They gradually withdrew from the Middle East back towards Central Asia. This led to a squabble between the grandsons of Genghis Khan with the Muslim brother attacking his nephew Hulegu, when he tried to exact revenge on the Mamluks. Kublai Khan eventually restored order, but there were significant dents in the Mongolian Empire both in the Middle East and in Southwest Asia.

Chapter Nine
The Decline of the Mongols in China

Section 1: Incompetence and Corruption

The decline of the Mongols in China was largely because of incompetent leadership. The empire began to shrink after the mid-1300s and once on the road to decline, it seemed unable to reverse the process. After Kublai Khan died, much of the leadership disintegrated into a disunited semi-feudal system. The Yuan dynasty weakened dramatically and the central government lost control of many of the Khanates, especially in Russia, the Middle East, and parts of Asia.

The populace hated the corruption and arrogance of the Mongolian elite and once Kublai Khan died, Toghon Temür Khan, a dissolute and sexually depraved man, was named his successor. He gathered together a close group, and they developed the Buddhist tantras into ceremonies that involved sexual orgies with men and women. They paid those who indulged in these homosexual practices handsomely.

As one can imagine, this kind of behavior had an effect on the morale of the populace, adding to the general neglect of the Empire, and helping to bring it to its knees.

Section 2: Collapse of the Mongol Empire

It had always been difficult for the Mongolians to look beyond the tribal structure, and there was no way that an extensive empire could be considered a large tribe, because it contained so many diverse cultures.

There was also discord when the Mongols entered the sedentary world instead of sticking to the nomadic way of life. Some factions resented the breakaway from their traditional culture while others began to practice the culture of the people they had conquered.

As a result, by 1260, the Mongol Empire had fallen into four distinct divisions. Kublai Khan ruled Tibet, Korea, China, and Mongolia. The next segment ruled Central Asia. The third was in West Asia and was called the Ilkhanids, centered around Baghdad. The final sector was the "Golden Horde," which was based in Russia and conflicted with the Ilkhanids for trade and grazing routes.

Section 3: The Final Years of Mongolian Empire in China

As the Yuan dynasty became weaker after the death of Kublai Khan, the leaders became increasingly aloof and more involved in Chinese than Mongolian culture. The Khans tried to control them by putting spies into rich households, forbidding gatherings, and forbidding the carrying of weapons. Ridiculous though it seems, only one carving knife was allowed among ten households. This must have made food preparation challenging.

A rebellion was finally arranged by a man, raised by a farm laborer who spent some years in a Buddhist monastery. He started a thirteen-year revolt by a group of peasant militants called The Red Turbans.

Despite harsh reactions to this revolt by the Mongol leadership, it could not control the sharing of innocent mooncakes that, like the modern-day fortune cookie, had hollow middles where information was passed on and instructions were given for attack in August 1368. The last Yuan Khan fled without defending his territory and was finally killed by Zhu Yuanzhang who founded the Ming dynasty.

Chapter Ten

The Collapse of the Mongol Empire in Russia, the Middle East, and Eurasia

Section 1: The Mongol Decline in the Middle East and Russia.

A usurper called Tamerlane or Timur, who claimed falsely to be a descendent of Genghis Khan invaded the Eurasian plain or steppes and roundly defeated the Golden Horde, who were a group of Mongols ruling over Russia and Ukraine, Moldova, Kazakhstan, and the Caucasus from the 1240s.

Although Timur died before he could see the full effects of the chaos he wrought, the Golden Horde was split into three, and they lost their control of the trade routes. While the Russians remained vassals of Mongolia from 1480, the Golden Horde was finally destroyed in 1503. The princes in Moscow colluded with their Mongol overlords until they became strong enough to challenge and defeat them, despite the Mongols burning down Moscow a few times in retaliation. The Mongol rulers in Russia were consistently weakened by rebellion and population integration until finally in 1552, Ivan the Terrible drove the last of the Khanates out of Russia.

The last descendent of Genghis Khan still reigning was deposed in Russia in 1783, when Catherine the Great annexed the last Mongolian population in Crimea. Nonetheless, the Mongolian influence on Russia remained significant. They also had a cultural influence called the Tatar heritage, which protected Russia from exposure to European cultural and political practices. Mixed-race Mongols and Turks were also called Tatars.

Over time, members of the Mongol Empire adopted the religion of those they conquered, which helped to assimilate them into local cultures and to break their bonds with Mongolia.

Section 2: The Unification of the Mongols under Tibetan Buddhism

It's always interesting to see how religion creates an enormous impact on a nation. In the mid-1500s, the Mongol lord Abtai Khan attacked China to win back territory. That was an abysmal failure, so he tried Tibet.

While busy with that campaign, he fell in love with Buddhism and gave the title Dalai Lama to the spiritual leader. It's a Mongolian word meaning ocean.

He built the Erdene Zuu Monastery, Mongolia's first major Buddhist center, which is now the world's oldest Buddhist monastery. Tibetan Buddhism, which was quite similar to traditional Mongolian shamanism, became the state religion of Mongolia.

To this day, there are strong links between Tibet and Mongolia. The fourth Dalai Lama was Mongolian and Mongolia gave military support to Tibet when Britain invaded in 1903. Mongolians still like to make a pilgrimage to Lhasa.

Section 3: What became of the Mongols?

The end finally came for the Mongolian Empire when they were subdued by the Qing dynasty in the 1600s, and Mongolia was made a province of China. The Mongolians fell back into their old nomadic tribal ways. There had been a major civil war in Mongolia in the early 1400s between the Khalkh and Oryat Tribes. When 60,000 Mongolians returned as the Empire folded, there was a period of resurgence. The Mongolians united again briefly under Esen Khan and attacked China and seized the Ming Emperor. China fought back four years later, and Esen Khan was killed. Mongolia fell back into its quasi-feudal combination of traditional living, squabbles, and skirmishes.

Etching of the Ottoman Mamluk lancers, early 16th century - The end finally came for the Mongolian Empire when they were subdued by the Qing dynasty in the 1600s, and Mongolia was made a province of China. The Mongolians fell back into their old nomadic tribal ways. There had been a major civil war in Mongolia in the early 1400s between the Khalkh and Oryat Tribes.

A 14th century CE illustration of Mongol mounted archers in battle.

The original artwork hangs in the National Library, Berlin.

Chapter Eleven
The Contributions of the Mongols to History

It's easy to accept the common thinking that Mongols were barbarians and plunderers who were intent simply to maim, massacre, and pillage. This understanding, based on Russian, Persian, and Chinese accounts of the ruthless speed and brutal lust for power that allowed the Mongols to develop the largest adjacent land empire in the history of the world, has molded both Western and Asian images of the Mongols and of Genghis Khan in particular, as ruthless, brutal barbarians who left a legacy of pain and suffering and decimated the world population.

In fact, the Mongols added considerable value to history.

1. During the reign of Kublai Khan, many great innovative thinkers, architects, and builders were employed to construct magnificent monasteries and temples. They sensibly realized their own cultural, scientific, and educational limitations and relied heavily on the more

sophisticated, more advanced civilizations, which they captured, to provide them with ideas, skills, and knowledge.

2. The Khans also invested in the development of astronomy and medicine and constructed great buildings. Notable is the Grand Canal in Beijing, Beijing itself, the Xanadu Summer palaces, and the Yam, their impressive postal and messenger system. The Yam made it possible for explorers, missionaries, and merchants to pass through wide tracts of the then-known world and find relatively safe lodging and refreshments.

3. Most important was the linking of Asia and Europe in a way that inextricably bound the East and the West. They created and fostered a positive relationship with foreigners and were largely tolerant of other cultures.

4. The Mongols allowed and encouraged travel, which opened up previously unknown areas to exploration, mapping, sharing of ideas, skills, philosophies, and most importantly, trade. The Silk Road proved invaluable in opening up the riches of the East to the West, and vice versa. This also inspired explorers to find a sea route to Asia

and was directly linked to the "golden age" of exploration in the 1400s.

5. The Mongols developed a written form of their language, which had previously been part of the oral tradition. This happened right at the very start of the Mongol Empire, possibly in 1204, when Genghis Khan captured a Uyghur scribe who was called Tata-tonga. He adapted the Uyghur alphabet into Mongol.

6. The Mongolian Khan encouraged religious tolerance, and Buddhism and Islam were strong among them. They also embraced and welcomed other cultures.

Of the many lessons one can learn from Mongolian history, it is that no empire builder or invader of other lands brings only harm. Nations learn from one another and develop into other, and often better, variations of themselves.

In conclusion, and in the words of Stefano Carboni and Qamar Adamjee of The Metropolitan Museum of Art, *"The legacy of Genghis Khan, his sons, and grandsons is also one of cultural development, artistic achievement, a courtly way of life, and an entire continent united under the so-called Pax Mongolica ("Mongolian Peace").*

And this puts the bloody history of the Mongolian Empire into some sort of perspective.

A Classic Example of Mongolian Architecture - The gate of the Yellow Palace in Khuree.

Chapter Twelve
Conclusion

What a fascinating story the history of the Mongolian Empire is. It reads like an epic novel with all the aspects of wide-open spaces, warhorses, ruthless men armed with arrows and spears, pillage, and chaos. It looks at the mystical worlds of Shamanism and Tibetan Buddhism. It exalts the building of the pleasure garden and palaces of the almost mythical Xanadu. It limps through the dreary utilitarian control of communism. It is a story of vast successes, one of the greatest feats of empire building ever known, and of depressing failure as it trudged to its end, over generations.

Like all great historic tales, the rise and fall of the Mongolian Empire has lessons to teach us all. It teaches us that growth comes from collaboration and assimilation. The Mongolians were unsophisticated people who wisely used the knowledge of the people they captured. They learned from the Chinese to make paper, to use a printing press, to develop tools like a triangular plow and a blast furnace, and, of great importance, in changing the face of warfare, to make gunpowder. The Mongols were the first to create hand grenades using these techniques.

It teaches us that tribal people find it difficult to develop national culture and form a centralized government. Every time a strong leader died, the Mongolian people resorted back to tribalism and in-house skirmishes. This ultimately affected the long-term success of the Mongolian Empire. We can see the enduring effects of tribal cultures in certain third-world countries today where people vote on tribal lines at the expense of the nation's best interests.

It teaches us that cooperation among different nations is the best way to foster growth, development, and invention. It's just unfortunate that this often comes about because of enforced cooperation such as through warfare and colonization. The effects of growth and positive change have to be weighed against the negative effects of lives lost or nations oppressed.

It teaches us that suppression of a large group of people, however harsh, will eventually lead to revolt and resistance even at the cost of personal safety. The Chinese peasant class revolted against the injustices imposed by the Mongolian Aristocracy. Few nations still exist where the suppression of the bulk of the population or certain groups within a population has not led to regime overthrow. Injustice eventually rankles until it cannot be borne anymore.

It also reminds us that human beings love to hear about colorful characters like Genghis Khan. They love an "against all odds" story where one-man defeats seemingly impossible odds to become a great hero, or as in the case of Genghis Khan, a great villain. Throughout history, colorful, terrifying, and larger-than-life characters have arisen and have appalled and fascinated us with their unthinkable deeds and adventures.

If nothing else, the history of the Mongolian Empire will have opened your eyes to a world that was possibly completely unknown to you or was just one line in a history book. When history becomes real, it can be a very satisfying adventure in its own right.

Chapter Thirteen
Discussion Question

Genghis Khan was a brutal villain without any compassion. He laid waste to the world that he conquered. What's your take on this? Please substantiate your answer.

Discussion Question

Kublai Khan was much more refined and cultured than his grandfather.

What do you think of this comment? Please substantiate your opinion?

Discussion Question

The Mongolian Empire collapsed because the leadership could not shake its tribal way of thinking. In what way would this have affected its long-term success? Is there any truth to this opinion?

Discussion Question

Do you think Genghis Khan really has 16 million descendants living today? How did the experts come up with this number? Do you believe this statistic?

Discussion Question

Mongolia had a particularly effective postal and messenger service. How would this have assisted its control over other nations? What other benefits might it have had?

Discussion Question

The traditional religion of the Mongol people was Shamanism. What do you understand by that term? What other early cultures were shamanistic? Do you know any modern-day people who believe in Shamanism?

Discussion Question

The Mongolian Khan encouraged religious tolerance, and Buddhism and Islam were strong among them. They also embraced and welcomed other cultures. Why do you think religious tolerance is important? Discuss.

Discussion Question

The Mongols developed a written form of their language, which had previously been part of the oral tradition. This happened right at the very start of the Mongol Empire, possibly in 1204, when Genghis Khan captured an Uyghur scribe who was called Tata-tonga. He adapted the Uyghur alphabet into Mongol. Why was it important for languages to transition from oral traditions to written ones? Share your thoughts.

Chapter Fourteen

Quiz Question

1. **True/False:** The Mongols were nomadic people who were exceptional horse riders. They lived in family groups. Their tent-like dwelling was called a yurt.

2. **True/False:** Genghis Khan was a great leader who led a siege on many other nations, but he was very compassionate. He tried to spare all of those he conquered. He was known as the "Benevolent Khan.".

3. **True/False:** Kublai Khan was the grandson of Genghis Khan. He invaded China and became emperor there. He built a palace called Xanadu.

4. **True/False:** The Mongolian forces tried to approach and capture Jerusalem. They were stopped by a group of Palestinian mercenaries. This was their third and final attempt. (False. They were stopped by the Mamluks who were a slave army on their first attempt and never tried again.

5. **True/ False:** The poem Kublai Khan was written by Samuel Coleridge. He wrote it after an opium-induced sleep. He never visited China.

6. **True/False:** The Dalai Lama was a Tibetan religious leader. His name was given by a Khan. It means Ocean.

7. **True/False:** The fall of the Mongolian Empire happened when they were invaded by an even more terrible army. They were completely routed. Almost the whole nation was slaughtered.

8. **True/ False:** Modern Mongolia is still greatly affected by communism. Nonetheless, it does not embrace communist principles. It prefers old nomadic philosophies.

Quiz Answer

1. True

2. False: He was thought to have killed some 40 million people.

3. True

4. False: They were stopped by the Mamluks who were a slave army on their first attempt and never tried again.

5. True

6. True

7. False: It collapsed gradually as the local populations rebelled, and the chieftains and warlords started to squabble against one another

8. True

Bibliography

- A Portrait of Genghis Khan. Wikipedia. https://commons.wikimedia.org/wiki/File:Genghis_Khan_crop.jpg. Razr Nation

- The Mongolian Empire. https://en.wikipedia.org/wiki/File:Mongol_Empireaccurate.png#filelinks. Onetwo1

- The Silk Road.https://www.britannica.com/topic/Silk-Road-trade-route#/media/1/544491/223159 Britannica.

- A Portrait of Kublai Khan. http://commons.wikimedia.org/. Wikimedia Commons.

- Etching of the Ottoman Mamluk lancers, early 16th century. By Daniel Hopfer - British Museum[1], Public Domain, https://commons.wikimedia.org/w/index.php?curid=4107509

- A 14th century CE illustration of Mongol mounted archers in battle. (National Library, Berlin). https://www.worldhistory.org/image/11455/mongol-warriors-in-battle/ Unknown

- A Classic Example of Mongolian Architecture - The gate of the Yellow Palace in Khuree. https://picryl.com/media/1913-the-gate-of-yellow-palace-in-khuree-60121e. Wikimedia

Bonus Downloads

*Get Free Books with **<u>Any Purchase</u>** History Hub*

Every purchase comes with a FREE download!

or Click Here.

Scan Your Phone to open QR code

Thank You For Reading

As an independent publisher

with a tiny marketing budget

we rely on readers, like you.

Click here to a brief review on Amazon

If you're receiving help from this book,

would you please take a moment to write a brief review?

We really appreciate it.

Simply scan QR Code with your Smartphone

www.ingramcontent.com/pod-product-compliance
Lightning Source LLC
Chambersburg PA
CBHW081933120726
47997CB00010B/3130